Digital Marketing:
The Complete Content Marketing Handbook For Small Businesses

7,783 words
By Deborah L. Killion
©2015 All rights reserved.

TABLE OF CONTENTS

WHAT IS CONTENT MARKETING?
DIGITAL MARKETING
TYPES OF CONTENT MARKETING
OUTSOURCING ARTICLES
TO BUILD AN EMPIRE
WHICH BLOGGING PLATFORM SHOULD YOU USE?
BUSINESS IS ABOUT RELATIONSHIPS
EBOOKS
CREATING VALUE IN YOUR MARKETING CAMPAIGNS
HOW TO GET STARTED
CREATING WINNING EXPLAINER VIDEOS
HOW TO USE VIDEO ONLINE
DON'T SKIMP ON QUALITY
THE POWER OF SOCIAL MEDIA
SOME FINAL THOUGHTS

INTRODUCTION TO CONTENT MARKETING

If you are reading this book, then you probably want to know about content marketing. I am a professional content marketer but I don't focus on marketing. I learned what I know about content marketing due to my work as a successful copywriter for small and large businesses online for the past two years. I am also a video producer and marketer, and own my own technology and media production business. So these things have put me in the middle of content marketing as well.

But I am also a business owner, so I understand the reasons you need to know about content marketing. As a business owner and online e-commerce site owner myself, I knew that I needed to find out as much as possible about content marketing in order to get my business noticed amongst the thousands of other similar businesses out there.

The good news is: Small businesses can be on the same playing field with large businesses by just knowing how to successful market your content online.

There are as many approaches to content marketing as there are platforms and channels to market your content on. That is perhaps why there is so much confusion about content marketing: it's hard to know which methods to use to maximize your efforts and start seeing a return on your investment.

A business can go into debt quickly putting your money in the wrong place when it comes to online marketing. That's why this book should help you to read about the various ways to successfully carry out a content marketing campaign and then you can apply the techniques you think will work best for you. The important thing is that you get the picture---the WHOLE picture, from creating your branding message, producing your video, using infographics, and even how to use Google Analytics to measure your progress as you go.

WHAT IS CONTENT MARKETING?

I always try not to insult the intelligence of the people who read my books. I realize I could be talking to a savvy 7-figure big business owner who already knows a lot about content marketing and just wants to pick up a few tips from a professional copywriter who has been in the middle of content marketing and could offer some extra insight. Or I might also be talking to someone who really doesn't have a grasp on what content marketing is. I'll assume I'm talking to a little bit of both, and some more in the middle of this spectrum. So bear with me if you already know what it is. But many don't. And to be honest, it took me a while to really put my finger on what it was too.

Bill Gates once said that, "Content marketing will be at the heart of everything we do online on the internet within a few years," and he predicted that in the 1980's! He has certainly been right, and it has been around for a long time now. But it is just now beginning to really take center stage in terms of the importance to a business's online success.

Bill also said that the "future millionaires of the internet will be involved in content marketing." Let's think about that statement for a minute. Who did he mean? Copywriters like me? I'm in the middle of content marketing. And while I do make a good side income (around $3,000 per month) in this process of writing rich content for businesses that drives traffic to their website, I am by no means a millionaire. So who did he mean with this statement? I'm not sure exactly and though Bill is on my Facebook, he is in Africa at the moment or somewhere getting the new Microsoft Office ready for mass production when Microsoft packages their Windows 10 (oops, your secret's out, Bill, sorry!) Yes, Bill Gates did come in out of the woodworks to help with the new Microsoft Office and I'm secretly glad he did. But anyway, I am going to guess who Bill was talking about is the online business owner who has learned how to handle content marketing to his advantage!

But to clarify things, let's start with a definition of content marketing.

Content marketing is a technique whereby various media, advertising strategies, and tools are used to draw attention to, increase the traffic of, and increase conversions of online websites.

This means it could involved a large number of techniques, including blogging, video marketing, the use of social media, infographics, online paid ad campaigns, or anything else that takes content and points people to your business. It can also be DONE in a wide variety of ways: SEO (search engine optimization), multiple videos, animations, explainer videos, Twitter, Facebook, and/or any combination of the above. So that's why it can get confusing and that's why I wrote this book: to try to iron out all of the options and organize it a bit so that you can plan your content marketing strategy.

DIGITAL MARKETING
(vs. Traditional Methods)

I actually came from the era of analog and print, and evolved into the digital platform along with many others who did this as the technology changed. I got a Bachelor's degree in Radio-TV Production and Performance from Arkansas State University in 1988. During the 80's we DID have some digital equipment (such as the teleprompter, digital processors, and such like), but digital formats were not the mainstream. Our final output in our productions were all on VHS or BETACAM, which is another ancient format that is all but forgotten in our digital age. I write a blog called "Media Creation in the Technology Age," in which I address all sorts of issuing surrounding this march to digital format, so check it out when you can if you'd like to learn more. It speaks primarily to producers and publishers, like myself, who have made it their careers to live and work in the digital media production industry and technology and gives helpful tips on how to meet the challenges of our digital age. This could be helpful to businesses too and I do consider businesses to be among one of my most important markets.

TYPES OF CONTENT MARKETING

Now that we have talked about the transition from analog to digital, and from traditional print methods, network TV and radio ads to the online world, let's talk about the specific tools that can (and should) be used in your digital marketing strategies. I am not saying that you should use every single one of these. I am just presenting the benefits of each one, so that you can decide for yourself which is best for your business. You can use them in a variety of ways either in isolation or with other methods. But it is usually to your benefit to use more than one. In fact, I've written various articles for businesses the past 2 years that illustrate the importance of streamlining your marketing efforts and using an integrated approach to your advertising strategy so that you get the benefits out of different methods, platforms, and strategies. Below are 9 of what I consider to be among the best digital marketing strategies in existence today which you can utilize to maximize your impact on a growing online digital and mobile audience.

ARTICLES

Articles are created for a number of different purposes, for research, to serve as background for an ad campaign, and numerous other reasons. But the primary reason articles are written and created for content marketing is *to drive traffic*. Underline that and memorize it. Driving traffic is what content marketing is all about. This does not mean that it is sales COPY. But the underlying purpose is to drive traffic, which hopefully will result in a sale, or at least a lead that will pay off some day in the future.

HOW ARE ARTICLES USED IN CONTENT MARKETING?

Articles can be used in a number of ways in content marketing. Some business owners choose to have posts written for ezinearticles.com. At one time, this was considered the best way to promote your site. Ideally, you write articles for ezine that link back to your site to increase traffic. This still works! But with so much competition out there, it is estimated that you would have to write about 3,000 such articles in order to increase your rankings significantly in the search engines. It is also argued that putting articles on ezine is not enough. I happen to agree with this idea. Ezine is great but you need to link from a variety of places on the web in order to really see the benefit of your article campaign.

OUTSOURCING ARTICLES

If you are a business owner and wish to increase the amount of power your site has with article marketing, you will want to consider outsourcing this. By finding dedicated writers that can do this for you, you save yourself a lot of time trying to do it yourself. I'm a writer myself, as well as a technology business owner, but I realize most business owners are not writers. You want to focus on your business. So I suggest to business owners that you go to high content sites such as Crowd Content or Getacopywriter.com where you will find very high-quality top-notch writers (I'm one of them) that you can pitch your work to. They understand what it takes to get your business noticed and they are skilled at using key words in ways that both Google and people appreciate. Over time, using such sources will pay off with increase traffic and conversions, leads, and other benefits.

TO BUILD AN EMPIRE

If you DO decide to take on the article marketing tasks yourself, more power to you! Just realize that it takes a very long time to build up your collection of articles, all with SEO (search engine optimized) content that the search engines will reward. Do it a little at a time and realize that you are creating an empire—a network of multiple articles that will link back to your website or blog with the ultimate goal being to increase your organic traffic. Remember that this has nothing to do with paid traffic or paid ads. That is another strategy that we will get into in a future section. For now, just focus on creating articles in your niche area that searchers will be interested in reading. Think of yourself as a mini-magazine that houses all of the information about your target niche area that anyone would want to know. Start small and build a day at a time. Over time you will start to see the results. Remember, you are building an empire and Rome "wasn't built in a day."

BLOGS

No book on content marketing can be written without making blogs a central part of its content. "Blog" literally means "web log" and it is simply a format for housing a log of activities, events, or information. The history of blogging is interesting. It has only been around for about 20 years but has recently caught on as the most influential factor in influencing buying decisions.

THE HISTORY OF THE WEB LOG

Blogging actually started with people posting their family vacations online with pictures and inviting people to comment. They discovered that people would return to see if they had posted anything new the next day and within a few weeks, they had gained quite a following. Over time, businesses began to realize the value of blogs and started incorporating them into their marketing plan as well. Then SEO came along and Google's Blogger.com blogging platform, which got instant search rankings just for being on Google's platform. And things grew exponentially.

Blogging has come a way since those early days. Search engines have come to love blogs and include them in the searches, which makes them more accessible to potential customers. Website owners may choose to house their blog on the same site as their website, or off site on another server. There are advantages to both which we discuss below.

ON-SITE BLOGS

The advantage to on-site blogs is the fact that people will see your blog while on your site and it may be easier for them to remember. As a result of this, they may return more often to read your updates. This will increase your readership over time and build your audience, resulting in increased traffic and conversions. The use of key words (SEO) on your site will increase traffic even further and result in repeat visitors. Some of these people will also share on social media, so it is the wise blog owner that puts an easy-to-find social media link on the blog as well. Having a blog on-site also means that people may read your blog, then return to the main website or sales page to purchase after reading the blog. This will happen more often if you have done a good job of explaining what you wanted to explain about your product or service you are talking about in the blog, or in the information you provide to your customer. Often, just having valuable information about a particular product or service, or some helpful tips, may be enough to turn a visitor into a buyer and a customer into a brand evangelist.

WHICH BLOGGING PLATFORM SHOULD YOU USE?

It really doesn't matter which blogging platform you choose to use for your blog, as long as it has the features you need. Blogger.com (as mentioned before) is owned by Google so you will get some instant traffic just from being on Google's platform. But WordPress.com is gaining popularity and is considered one of the best blogging platforms now, because of its ability to be integrated with pretty much any web server. There are many other formats for blogging available. Many web servers have an integrated BLOG option within their web design platform as well. But remember, if you want on OFF-SITE blog to pull in traffic from other sources, you will need an off-site blogging solution. CreativeBloq.com has several blogging solutions in one of their on site
articles that will give you more insight into the platforms for blogging available today.

OFF-SITE BLOGS

There are advantages to off-site blogs too. Having an off-site blog will catch traffic that you would not get otherwise, if your blog was located on your main site URL. It will attract people who are just searching for a particular product or who want information on a certain niche area. This is your chance to nab some external traffic and increase your organic search power by locating your blog in a different location from your website. It also gives you an opportunity to increase traffic coming from another server or search engine by putting your key words out there with links back to your site. This increases your ranking with Google because Google views links back to your site as a sign that your site is popular with visitors. And it will be, if you provide meaningful content that people can benefit from.

WHAT SHOULD YOU PUT ON YOUR BLOG?

Some businesses wonder what they should put on their blog. You can do your blog any way that you choose, but he key is to offer something of value to your visitors. If you offer meaningful content, customers will appreciate it and return often to see what you will post next. It also increases your credibility with visitors and gains you followers. These can turn into leads that you can send email newsletters to later on.

So, when considering what to put on your blog, think about what your target audience would want to read about and focus on that. Example: If you have a car mechanic's business, what types of topics would your readers want to see? Here are a few possibilities:

1. How to Change the Oil in your car
2. 5 Ways to tell if your Transmission if Going Bad
3. 7 Money-making Tips on Car Repairs

Well, you get the idea. Consider giving your customers something free (information they can use) and they will often consider you first when they need car repairs. See how it works? You might call this indirect selling, but it is just basic business sense too that we often saw back in the "old days." No, I'm not old enough to remember but my grandparents often told me about someone fixing a flat tire for them free of charge without asking anything in return or a doctor making a house visit and not even sending a bill. These types of what I call "PRO BONO" (a legal term meaning 'free') jobs can often come back a hundredfold in the form of future sales, simply because you took the time to do something out of the goodness of your heart for them.

BUSINESS IS ABOUT RELATIONSHIPS

Stephen Covey, the now famous author and professional presenter and author of the series, "7 Habits of Highly Effective People" often says that he thinks business is about relationships, not things. And I agree. Sure, you can get someone to buy something once from you. But will they be back? Relationships are built with trust, just like any other type of relationship. So, when you offer people something of value without asking anything in return, you are depositing a positive dividend into a customer's account. And like any investment, it will come back to you over time, if you nurture it.

A FINAL WORD ABOUT BLOGS

So when considering what to put on your blog, think about your target audience and what they would like to see. Make it interesting and engaging first, and focus on SEO (key words) second. Then focus on building relationships with your posts. Encourage interaction and sharing and build your audience. Make sure to include media (such as pictures, infographics, and video) to encourage more sharing and engagement.

PRINT BOOKS

With the emphasis on ebooks these days, it might be easy to forget the importance of print books. As a business, having print books on your topic or niche area puts the information directly in the hands of potential customers and can generate discussions on your business both off and online. Print is more permanent and tangible than ebooks. People can actually get their hands on it, turn the pages and feel connected to what you are saying on a more real level. No one can deny the convenience and power of digital media. That's what I specialize in! But there is still a value to print, at least for now and I hope that it will stay around for a long, long time.

One place you need to continue to use the print medium for is in direct marketing such as mailers, postcards, flyers, and such like. Many businesses now use print media as a way to connect with more potential customers with their online digital advertising. For example, sending a flyer about your new product is great, but why not include a website address where they can get 10% off just for going to the website. Online coupons are hugely popular with customers and will get you more business. In addition, you may create more loyal customers by implementing coupon programs, reward programs, and other incentives through print media that you cannot do online. Now that the advent of digital media is here, you should use it to its fullest, as it has the most potential for worldwide reach. But don't forget the print mailers and direct mail campaigns, which is still considered by Fortune 500 companies to be the #1 tool they have to reach the masses on a single ad campaign. When you do use this medium though, make sure and tie it to your digital marketing campaigns too.

EBOOKS

It would be difficult to communicate to my readers just how important ebooks are today. The very fact that you are reading this indicates that you agree and you are experiencing this phenomenon on a personal level. Hopefully my ebooks give you something of value that you can take away from the experience and apply to your life or business. I actually came from a "classic literature" background, preferring the works of such greats as Edgar A. Poe, William Shakespeare, Thoreau and Emerson over Danielle Steele or Stephen King. This classic background seems hardly relevant to many today who don't understand the power of it. But because I was exposed to and started writing very much like authors such as Poe and others, I became a top writer in every single content site I am involved with, and in high demand from multiple clients.

My point with this is that if you think and aim high in your standards and create value for your readers, they are going to want to read your message and even come back for more. This doesn't mean that your ebooks have to sound like some modern-day rendition of an Emily Dickinson poem or one of Emerson's intellectual essays! But keep quality in mind no matter what your message is and you will create an ebook that will serve you well.

Probably for most of you reading this, your goal is not to become an established ebook author. You likely want to use your ebook as a free giveaway in order to promote your business in multiple places, or send it as an extra in your email newsletters. No matter what the reason, think about how you can add value to your ebook. Give readers and customers something they need.

HOW TO CREATE VALUE

In order to create value in your ebook, think about what your customers want. You probably know your customers more than I ever could. Go back in your customer service log or think about the most recent customer service call or email you got. What were customers wanting? Were they happy with the service your company gave them? Why or why not? Think of things they have addressed in customer service communications in the past, pull things from conversations you've had with your clients and customers, and think about how you can give them answers to their questions or a solution to their problem in the ebook. Most of all, conclude by helping them see that your business has the best solution for them, by providing a call to action at the end to encourage engagement. Ebooks can be a very effective promotional tool that you offer customers as something free that they will see as valuable and later they may reciprocate by making a purchase.

WHERE TO MARKET YOUR BUSINESS EBOOK

As mentioned before, if you are a business owner, CEO, or business manager, chances are your goal is not to make money on the book. Instead, you probably want the eBook to serve as a tool to generate leads and engage people who might not otherwise be engaged in your material or your business. This means that you do not necessarily need to publish your eBook on Amazon, Barnes & Noble, or iTunes. All you need to do is save it as a PDF file and send it out en masse to your email list! It's that simple.

HOW TO GET STARTED

If you've never written an eBook, I've put the steps below that anyone can follow to get you to where you need to be so that you'll know you have it in the right format. But how you create your eBook is totally up to you. Amazon Kindle actually accepts several formats but they prefer Microsoft Word. Even if you have no plans to put your book in Amazon Kindle (or any of the other eBook markets), Microsoft Word is the standard for creating an eBook so I do highly recommend this.

STEPS TO CREATING AN EBOOK

Here are the steps to creating an eBook, no matter whether you plan to put it in an online market or just put it online for users to download, or to send in your company emails:

1. Brainstorm topics you think your users will appreciate and need. Base this on your customer service emails, phone calls, and other interactions you have had with customers. Listen to their concerns. Answer their questions. Use your ebook as a way to communicate something permanent to your loyal customers, or as an incentive to get new customers. If you answer their questions, they will read it.
2. Narrow your topic. This is a practice done by professional writers but it applies to anyone who writes an ebook. Remembering that you cannot be everything to everyone is the single most important thing you should do in order to leverage the power of a digital book as a marketing tool. This helps you target the people most likely to buy from you.
3. Write down about 10 headings. These will be your "chapters" that you will address in your ebook. Keep in mind this is not an absolute rule. You can make the ebook as many chapters are you want. But writing down headlines gives you direction in where you want to go with your ideas and takes the reader through the eBook in a logical progression. It also gives you an outline so that you can stay on track and know when you've covered everything you wish to cover.
4. Open a Microsoft Word document and start writing. Always think about what your reader wants or needs as you write. What would they find valuable related to your business? You also want to think about what it would take to get them to take action by coming to your business to solve their problems. But don't make the eBook itself "salesy." I've written for hundreds of businesses for their blogs and websites and I've learned how to avoid the sales pitch, while still leading readers to the opinion that the business is the only one to help them. This takes skill and I've gotten good at it these 2.5 years that I've been a professional copywriter. If you want me to help you with this, you can contact me at: thestudiobydeb1@gmail.com and I may be able to write your ebook for you, or at least help you with your blog copy. I am

still taking on independent writing jobs as of this writing, though I've had to slow down a bit on how many jobs I take on due to my technology and media business and my national magazine pitches, etc. and my independent projects. But do contact me if you need help and I will do my best to help you out. I'm a former educator turned entrepreneur and I really enjoy helping fellow businesses succeed in the online marketplace. And eBooks and blogs are two of the very best ways to do this.

5. Create your title page. You'll need the first page to have the title at the top, then space down (this does NOT have to be perfect), and type your name and put the © symbol if you wish to acknowledge that you own the copyright, so others cannot freely post or reproduce it. Put the date after this that you are publishing the ebook. For purposes of publishing, consider the date that you started sharing the eBook, even if you just plan to send it through email to potential clients.

6. Skip a page. You know how business documents sometimes have a blank page and at the bottom are the words: "This page intentionally left blank." Well, this is what you are doing here, but don't write that sentence I just wrote above. I have always thought that was a crazy thing to put, and defeats the purpose too, I might add! Anyway, just leave one page blank. Then on the next page, create a table of contents.

7. Create a table of contents. This part is a bit more difficult but all you need to do really is just create **BOLDED HEADINGS** at different places (preferably at the tops of pages) that you wish to serve as your 'chapters.' Then create your table of contents on the third page of your eBook in which you list the name of the title. It can be the same as the BOLDED heading. Highlight the title you call it in the TOC then hit the "LINK" button at the top of MS Word and you should see a list of all of the BOLDED HEADINGS you created. Choose the one you want. MS Word will automatically create a link to that chapter. What this does is to create an automatic "jump to" command so that when readers select a specific chapter in your book, they can go right to it, rather than scroll all the way down time and time again to get to the information they need. Save your readers

time and they will reward you. Besides, most people probably will not read your entire eBook anyway, especially if you are writing on a variety of subtopics. Customers tend to be looking for specific information and once they find what they need, they move on. Make it easy for them. If you need additional help on creating a table of contents, I recommend you go here: https://kdp.amazon.com/help?topicId=A1JMIOQ2RP4DPK. Even if you do not plan to publish your eBook on Kindle, it is a good idea to use Amazon Kindle as a standard in the formatting, since it is recognized as the worldwide standard on digital eBook publishing.

8. Save your finished work as a MS Word .doc, .docx, and .pdf. PDF is the standard for ebooks that you will send via email or post for download on your website or blog, etc. But also keep a copy of your MS Word document so that you can easily go in and make changes to your book later. You may or may not have a PDF editing tool and this costs extra money. If you only plan to make one eBook, there's no need to speed extra money. Just save each copy that you update as both a Word and PDF document, Word for your own safekeeping and PDF for your readers. Then keep it in a safe place so that you'll be able to send it as an attachment to your subscribers or put it on your website as a download. If you need help in how to offer a PDF file online on your website, I can help you with that too. I charge $50 per hour of work. Email me if you need my assistance with this and I'll see what I can do: thestudiobydeb1@gmail.com.

ONE FINAL WORD ABOUT EBOOKS

Ebooks are one of the best ways to get the word out about your business, company, or brand. I've been helping businesses do this for over 2 years now and I have written blog posts, ebooks, and web copy for these people. They later reported to me that it brought them more traffic than anything they have done and thanked me for my work. I am always glad to help businesses thrive. I understand the challenge of businesses regarding online marketing because I am not just a writer, I am a business owner as well. I'm not writing this ebook to get more business. Believe me, I'm busy enough, but again, if I can help you, contact me and I'll see what I can do. Alternately, if you don't have time to writer your own eBook, you can contract this work out to other writers at sites such as: http://crowdcontent.com, a very high-quality writing site with only top-quality writers and http://getacopywriter.com, an Australian-based writing content site which also emphasizes very high quality from professional writers. Unlike a lot of people in the content business, I do not recommend the "freelance sites," simply because it is a bidding war many times and you do not always get the quality you pay for. I've worked both sides of this, so I highly recommend using the above writing sites or similar content sites who focus on writing copy exclusively and offer you a larger ROI regarding your copywriting budget.

BROCHURES

Brochures are like a dinosaur in a modern world. They still exist but no one seems to know what to do with them any more. Local businesses use them for customers who come in their store. Some send them in mailers to others who might be interested in their services but who live further away. But few realize the potential of this "old world" method on a larger scale. I have written a few articles in my journey as an internet content marketer and freelance writer for direct mailing companies. In these articles, I talked about how companies are using brochures and postcard mailers to send out their information to thousands of people at once, using either the U.S. Postal Service's EDDM (Every Door Direct Mail) campaign or some similar marketing technique through mailing lists with companies like Vistaprint.com or others. These types of mass mailing direct mail campaigns get your message in the hands of the most people as fast as possible and can have a huge impact on a business's bottom line and ROI.

RESEARCH & CASE STUDIES

There's nothing like research and 'case studies' to back your business product or ideas that gets the attention of more people and builds your credibility. If you are not already a big name brand, you can put important research studies and names behind you to back up your ideas that can significantly increase the amount of credibility and punch you have in a competitive online market. You can insert these case studies in your blogs, with links back to the study itself, cite magazines which carry a lot of clout such as Entrepreneur or Forbes magazine (I've written for Forbes 3 times by the way), and you can even present your business product or concept to some of these online publications with a high following and see if they will link back to you. This can go a long way toward building your brand and your authority in an ever-increasing market of people looking for information.

NEWSLETTERS

Newsletters are the staple product of many online businesses that is free. That is, it is one of the best ways to gain followers, potential customers, even vendors and other people who can contribute to the growth of your business. It is easy to set up. Simply create a form through your web server to allow people to enter their name and email address and ask them to put SUBSCRIBE in the body so you'll know they wish to subscribe to your email list. This is not only a great way to keep people informed of what you are doing in your business, but also serves as a great leads capturing service as well. All you need is their email and this tells you legally that they want information. From this, you can build a huge database of people that are interested in what you have to offer and these are your best candidates for future customers. Plus, they may share it with others if they believe that what you offer has something of value to them. (See Social Media Links section).

Author's Note: The below section is especially for the benefit of my students on Udemy.com, to further educate them on the different types of videos used in effective video marketing campaigns. But it will be of benefit to anyone wanting to launch a successful video marketing campaign, whether a small business or a multi-level corporation. The rules are the same, and it works at any level.

EXPLAINER VIDEOS

I have written multiple articles on this topic and I am also a video producer so this is a topic close to my heart (and pocketbook). Videos are the single most important factor in conversions. When people are out there looking for information on a product they are considering purchasing, they are 65% more likely (as of this writing) to purchase after having viewed a video on the product. When you compare the actions of customers who simply see an ad for a product and those who view a video before purchasing, the difference is obvious. The videos do not even have to be a "sales pitch" in order to convert. You simply explain what the product does, what it can do for their lives (save them time, money, help them in some way), or solve a problem they have. By doing this, you answer the questions they are looking for in answer to some issue they need a solution for and this is often enough to convert to a sale.

Explainer videos can also be used in the following contexts:
- As a corporate video to announce upcoming products or services or about policies and official information regarding your company
- For branding- Explainer videos help you to get your brand out to a larger number of people and keep your company's presence in the consciousness of more potential buyers.
- As a Training video- You can use explainer videos to teach new employees or staff members what you expect of them on the job, or lead them through a series of steps that teach them the daily tasks that they are required to do on the job.
- As a Sales Presentation- Explainer videos can also be used as a sales technique in which you explain the reasons why your product, service, or business idea is beneficial to them.
- For any other reason- Explainer videos can be used to roll out a new product, to explain a process or idea your company has, as a way to communicate with B2B partners, employees, or online collaborators, and numerous other people that are involved in the process of your business.

HOW TO USE VIDEO ONLINE
(*for my Udemy students)

I could write an entire book just on how to use video online. Video marketing is one of the most effective tools that you can utilize to increase the impact of your message, promote your brand, and draw people to your site that you could possibly find. There are also many techniques that I have learned to use, such as cross-referencing videos to each other, placing strategic keywords in the video descriptions on YouTube, and numerous other methods. I plan on creating some instructional videos in the near future on how to do all of this, so keep an eye on http://smalltownglobal.com for more information in the near future. We are also adding media to our online webstore at: http://www.smalltownglobal.com/apps/webstore/products/category/980774?page=1 which features numerous ebooks on the topic of marketing and content strategies so be sure to check this out too.

Click below to take my course on Video Marketing on Udemy.
https://www.udemy.com/video-marketing-for-small-businesses/?instructorPreviewMode=guest

There are about as many ways to use video as there are places to put the videos on the web today. Use them in blogs to accent your blog posts, use them on your main website to increase audience engagement, post them on social media (See Social Media section), in emails as an incentive to click on your ad, and many more.

The goal with video is to make people stop and take notice and video does that automatically. Text is considering boring in and of itself, but video is dynamic. It's 3-dimensional. It gets people excited about what you are saying. The best thing about video is that you don't need a multi-million-dollar budget to create a video. You can do it yourself with a digital video camera and some video editing software, or outsource it to any number of freelance video producers which you can find on such sites as Odesk.com, Elance.com, (which is now owned partly by Amazon), as well as many other freelance or independent contractor sites. Fiverr.com is growing in popularity as a good place to get freelancers as well. As an independent contractor, I do not do much work on there due to the low price point, as I am trying to market myself as a high-quality highly-paid producer and writer, etc. but if you find a good one on Fiverr, you can keep your budget on video production amazingly low using their services.

DON'T SKIMP ON QUALITY

One final word on video production and marketing. Don't skimp on quality. You can do it yourself if you or someone on your staff is skilled at this, using a "talking head" type video that you do in which you are simply telling people how to do something or presenting some aspect of your business that you want them to know about. But just make sure the editing is done well so that the result is professional. This is especially true if you are doing a corporate video, but any explainer or informational video should be done with the highest standards possible. I learned what I know through both my formal education in Radio-TV Production and on my own through experimentation and through having my own technology and media production business in my hometown. If you don't have any one else to do your video and you would like me to try to help, you can contact me. I cannot take on every project, but I consider businesses one of my primary markets and I do try to help businesses with their video marketing when I can. My current rate is $50 per hour. Contact me if you are interested in my services or just go to http://smalltownglobal.com to sign up for my updates if you think this is something I can help you with in the future. I am moving more toward a product business model (digital products, media, and technology) rather than a service industry, but I will continue to write content for blogs and produce audio and video for select clients as I have time. My content writing and marketing will remain a very central part of my business when I officially launch Small Town Global in 2016 and beyond.

PODCASTING

You could say that podcasts are the audio version of video marketing and they have been growing in popularity greatly in recent years. Developed initially as a way to listen to audio clips at a later time via an iPod, Apple and other key players in the technology field helped raise the awareness of this technology through the launch of iTunes primarily, as well as other platforms which were topic-centered and niche-focused. Since then, sites such as Soundcloud have emerged as a way for businesses, artists, authors, musicians, or anyone with a mission can broadcast their ideas to the world. Soundcloud also works with app development software so that you can actually pull in audio feeds from their platform to serve as an audio stream for the app or media project. Soundcloud allows either listening "on the fly" from their site or downloading clips and they have both a free and paid version so that you can increase your options. This is a great way to increase your brand's impact for those who come in from their platform and you have the ability to share the podcasts you create and upload with multiple platforms as well.

THE POWER OF SOCIAL MEDIA

No ebook on digital content marketing would be complete without discussing social media. Some millionaire entrepreneurs on the popular show, "Shark Tank" state that their income and revenue is generated by social media alone sometimes topping in the millions. Social media is one of the top strategic ways to channel your ad dollars into the sales funnel with the least amount of investment and come out on top. Your return on investment, dollar for dollar, will be right on target if you focus on social media as one of your main strategies and platforms. Facebook and Twitter have millions of views per month and this number is only expected to increase over the next few years.

CONCLUSION: AN INTEGRATED APPROACH

We have talked a lot in this ebook about the various types of marketing, which should hopefully give you more insight on the arsenal of tools that you have at your fingertips to utilize for effective digital marketing campaigns. We spent a lot of time on video marketing, in particular, because, as both a video producer and business owner, as well as a highly-paid content writer who is in the middle of this, I know the importance of video in your ad campaigns. You will get the highest level of ROI (return on investment) though by streamlining these efforts in some systematic way, and *combining the best* of them together to best serve your needs. For example, don't just do a marketing video. Instead do a marketing video and put it in your blog, website, and Facebook page. Don't just create a podcast. Shout it to the world on Twitter. Some of what I am talking about is just good promotion and marketing techniques. But it also involves using a variety of platforms and mediums to get your point across. What I'm referring to really is meeting people "where they are," on different platforms, so that you find your audience through whatever channels they are using to get their information, entertainment, and enjoyment.

SOME FINAL THOUGHTS

Integrating media just takes a "bird's eye view" of what people are doing online, what platforms they use (you know most of them from reading this ebook), and then taking a streamlined approach to putting your videos and digital ads out there to the masses. Only by looking at all of the different types of digital marketing available to you, including the multiple platforms where people come in, the devices they use, and the behaviors they exhibit online, can you get a true picture of where and who your target audience is, then broadcast your message to them where they are.

Planning is everything when it comes to a digital marketing campaign. Start small and build as your budget allows, and always remember it is better to take one small step than to do nothing. As long as you are moving forward with ideas, you can't be sitting still.
-Deborah L. Killion, writer & entrepreneur/media producer

"One small step for man….one giant leap for mankind." –Neil Armstrong

Please go to my website and blog and visit Amazon Kindle and Audible.com to get the full benefit of my books and ideas. I plan to put out many more soon so be watching.
Website: http://smalltownglobal.com
Blog: http://smalltownglobal.blogspot.com
Email: thestudiobydeb1@gmail.com
Happy sailing!

THE END

www.ingramcontent.com/pod-product-compliance
Lightning Source LLC
Chambersburg PA
CBHW070224210526
45169CB00024B/1538